Public works

POEMS | RONNA BLOOM

Public Works

POEMS | RONNA BLOOM

Pedlar Press | Toronto

ACKNOWLEDGEMENTS

The publisher wishes to thank the Canada Council
for the Arts and the Ontario Arts Council for their
generous support of our publishing program.

CANADIAN CATALOGUING IN PUBLICATION
DATA

Bloom, Ronna, 1961-
    Public works / Ronna Bloom.

Poems
ISBN 0-9732140-2-3

I. Title

PS8553.L665P82 2004   C811'.54   C2004-
903809-5

First Edition

Designed by Zab Design & Typography, Winnipeg

Printed in Canada

Public Works

CONTENTS

Skin and Bones

Public Works

Public Works

WHAT WORKS

Index

Air. The art gallery and bank (Montreal, Canada, Greece on the Danforth, Korea on Bloor Street).

Bicycles (falling) and birds and beef and buses on Christie Street.

Carr (Emily). Cedar tree, cedar pole.

Cemetery, *Consolatrix Afflictorum*. (The stone virgin on a hill of sage, stations below. Climb down to the parking lot, a handful of fruit.)

Chocolate.

Cows and customs (if a cow falls on your land, who is responsible?).

Deer (dead), electricity, gas, God, Ginsberg (to ease the pain of living).

Gown, hospital, hydro. Hyrtl Skull Collection. Food (another inventory: duck, beef, deer, bread, white, milk, eggs).

Inspections, law, legislature (that building in the middle of a circle owned by a tower), library (the subway under its tables).

Lunetti (Adoration of the Shepherds) and marriage (their bodies shine).

Military (epaulettes, suits, pinstripes), monastery (in a circle), news.

Neighbourhood nursing homes. Ontario. Paintings, parking tickets, paramedics (Ken and Pete), poems.

Queen's Park, Queen Street Mental Health, radiation, red, Rothko.

Solid house (all our houses are imaginary).

South, subway, Sunnybrook shuttle bus, summons, synagogue, syringe.

Tattoo (a painting on skin or wall: eyeliner at the top of the CN Tower, blinking).

Teacher (Ms. Martin, Ms. V. singing), tenor, tent (flapping, flapping, all my tent pegs banged in).

Trees (bloom), underground, voltage.

Demographics

men and women, teachers, hospital workers, politicians, people who shop at Loblaws, cake bakers, people who are retired, vulnerable, lost, who don't know the names of things, pretzel eaters, artists, people who've been to any kind of gallery, who ride bicycles, subways, people who walk on oily gravel roads, get parking tickets, pay, have fallen in love with paramedics, people who are intimate with the mouths of flowers, people compelled to watch the academy awards disgusted, who watch news on television, people who want attention without saying so, whose bodies fill with anxiety like a liquid, who love something that won't leave them and something that will, warriors who take vitamins, ambivalent people, scared people who do things, anyone willing.

Body and Soul

EACH BEAK POINTED AT ITS OWN PATCH OF SKY

The world is a big tree
and the birds come, rest on its branches.

This bird, a right branch,
this bird, a left.

Leaves shimmer in the round air
and the birds, on their branches, stare.

From behind two layers of glass, I see them
and they look alike.

Hey bird, I want to shout,
One of your friends is two branches over!

They are twitching their heads in opposing directions,
each beak pointing and alone.

Then a grey cat lands
on the wall across
making an ancient sound
and the birds swim down
in a single motion, diving
out of this world.

LAST DOCK OF SUMMER

In this sloped week
among the docks of summer
I write endings. Difficult letters
with words rushing. Or blacked out.
The jagged plunge of dash and stop and sigh.
I look up. The window
is a clear and open envelope to the lake
and no one is here with me. Only the loons
and in their wake, the boats
sliding up and down, only the clock
and the ritual walk to town
for a coke.

Otherwise I am quietly writing.
And lately no poems but these
letters of *I miss you* and
Thank you. I'm tired and *Goodbye.*
Accumulated losses — selves —
pile up behind me like summer fruit.

Today I wrote those letters and lay them
beneath the window like cooling pies. These are my goodbyes.
The last dock of summer smells cooked, baked down
jammy, smells of water.

Now on the edge of swimming, toes curled
clamped on August. Diving or not diving.
Go don't go, the loons cry.
The lake is already fall
at another fathom.
There is another season
where no one I know is.
I stand on the dock,
this one thin finger
of wood and air.

CRAYOLA MANDALA

I am drawing with the stubby brown
and purple, the softened red,
the creamy black. Drawing circles
in the centre of each five-inch square
filling them with rings or else spirals.
I like to carry crayons
in case of emergency.
I am filling in colour with no teacher
but what soothes,
a moving hand and no words.

Is it those
circles or those colours, or
the wider circle of the day — the sun,
the bells, the meals, the work,
the bells, the meals, the night, the sun?
There's a roundness
in my heart the shape of a hug
and no one keeps coming in.

Each time I suggest a body
it doesn't fit.

So I just keep feeling no one here,
the ring of my heart
encircling no one.

MENDICANT LOVE

In the prayer house, bent over, the back
of your grey head unkempt, hair
looser than your usual, unimpeachable,
unfrayed looks. You've let yourself go.

Here to celebrate family joy. In the row
of husbands. Which joy is it?
Rocking forward
body bent in giving over.
I have seen you bent further still
for the digging of your own kin grave,
you, in your fine combed suit.

The rough
body of your youth, the beaten
unpraised body of your ghetto years
comes forward in times like these.
Forgive me for noticing.
The polished and pressed
silk body of you, untouched,
curled back into itself, is a clutch
of its own, a busy grip of devotion
and prayer.

Standing here in the back
higher up and apart,
from this perspective I can see you more

your shoulders beginning to soften and round.
Do it, it's your melting I want.
I too carry that devotion
to something inhuman,
a perfection that is cold
irreproachable
that threatens to save us.
It's not God that's the problem
it's how we raise up the rules
higher than our heads
and call out to them.

TWO KINDS OF LIGHT

1.
Hers is a lamp.
A table lamp in the room of handed down
furniture: the papier mâché table with mother-
of-pearl, oak cabinet, a shapely armature
to hold old things. In the house's heart,
among tall trees and the shade
of other houses, the room is shrouded,
the lamp perpetually on. Yellow.

2.
He strains toward sun,
unshapes the room the lamp yellows.
Tears walls out, as with ceilings, roofs, to make
more windows, break in sky,
hack through to outside light
to white, the way a man
having a heart attack grabs at his shirt
rips it open for air, gasps, *more light!*

3.
His need to be freed is her need, feared.
Instead she says *I'll provide the bulb.*
I'll provide the walls, he says. All seems fine.
But the one with walls can't breathe,
and the one with bulb also weakens, can't see
in the dimness. Goes out and chops down a tree.
There is air in the room, sky and a bulb. Two kinds of light.
There may even be a house. It opens on hinges.

CONFESSIONS OF A DOMESTIC NOUN

Forgive me roosters
for thinking you chickens,
for not recognizing the combs in your hair.

Forgive me Pines
for calling you Spruce, for giving
up and calling you *trees*.

How would I like
to be any old noun
in one of your poems?

Forgive me wildflowers
not knowing your names
(I picked you anyway, I liked you best).

Forgive me glassy web, biting stone
upsetting you on every walk.
For me, going out into the world

is not coming home.
Like you, I'm unknown
in plain sight.

THEIR BODIES SHINE

1. Dust

I sponge dust off the low pine table, lifting
the framed photograph of my old friend
now moved away. I wipe the cherubs
on Aunt Florence's lamp, getting in the crooks
of their small brass elbows,
bent to hold up crowns of leaves, their bodies
shining in lamplight. The teapots
from India and China, gifts from travellers,
their dust I ignore. I wipe the plate
from the Jordans, neighbours in Ireland
who smoked their own bacon,
Mr. Jordan a butcher in England before
moving west with eleven children.
I watched him kill two chickens
with tiny cracks of the neck. I remember
his wellington boots in the mud as he
lay the chickens down. "For the wedding next week,"
he said, "we're going to slaughter a beast."
The father gave his daughter away,
the daughter, her place.
The cow gave muscle, gristle, her body, meat.
At the height of the night in the mended hall
the ten sisters danced: a ring of trees, holding hands.
The brother, small stoic
usher, kept quiet at the back. We exchanged the day's

blessings. Nodding. They gave me
this plate when I left Ireland,
its viney flowers and scalloped edge.
Dust actually has a smell if you leave it long enough.

II. Ether

Her brother is dying. Lies out there
on the Queensway and nothing
she can do will stop it.

She, herself, dissolving
into the family ether. How we
disappear
after the ones we love, we go too

III. Stars

My eyes like damp sponges
soak them in. My bare feet
clean from the shower on the cold grass.
Behind the house in my sleep shirt,
no underwear,
just one quick look.

HOUSE

Where a solid house
once stood
a wholly fictitious image
cuts in, just as if
the whole thing existed
completely in the brain.
— RAINER MARIA RILKE, *Duino Elegies,*
Seventh Elegy

There was a cake, for sure
a gleaming cake with candles;
there was a fridge she urged me open;
there was a visit, weekly to her house
that held a fridge, a cake;
there was a clear patch. Now
for sale, a flattened barn, the house
burnt to its cement foundation
three cement front steps.
There was a kitchen with a cake
there was a solid house
and Mrs. Pelletier waiting for me there
glad I'd come
with what a twelve-year-old has to say.
Now no plan but just my footsteps.
Now no house just that patch,
land and this fictitious twelve-year-old
solid as a house.

I go around the back (there is no back),
and take a shit. I have to go, and what else
is there to do? Was it really still a house, a happiness?
Perhaps this act a mark of desecration
but there *is* no house — just flattened boards
drainpipes scorched and curling. A sink.
Hard to link this with the house I'd visit weekly
warm kitchen, gaslit stove and Mrs. Pelletier.
Open the fridge, she urged.
Oh, the disbelief, without a more ordained relation
that she'd expect me, so much so she made a cake.
There was a cake and a foundation, there was
her waiting for me there,
now a protest for nothing left
but land. There was this twelve-year-old
and the gleaming cake itself,
which, I know,
there was.

BLUE WINDBREAKER

You go out in your blue windbreaker
get on your bike. Someone sees you and waves:
a neighbour. In the store, the owner
sells you milk, gives change, says, *Thank you.*
You ride away. This is as much as can be
remembered when your friend wonders the next day
why you didn't turn up, why you haven't
called. He calls your house but you live alone
and so, obviously, no one is home. He comes by
and knocks. No. He knocks
at the neighbour's, asks
if she's seen you. No. But yesterday.
Says she saw you on your bike
in your blue windbreaker.
Your friend goes back to work, calls you later and
you don't answer. The neighbour sees your cat
at the window. Other friends call your sister
then your mother. They begin coming over,
ring the neighbour who says I'm worried and goes in.
Nothing's changed. But the cat is lonely.
Did you know you were going somewhere? Did you plan
a secret escape, a private elopement?
Your friends want to think so. They want to know
that you planned this so they can be angry.
Unmarrying your life.
Otherwise they are staggering into work,
onto subways and roads,
lost like you.

CADILLAC

I am falling off my bicycle
barely tipping
into the intersection.
But the shame of falling — almost falling —
mixed with some anger I've been feeling
makes me swear in the street
and throw down my bike
almost stepping back into traffic
when a car horn blares and a man in black cadillac
wags his finger at me, a chiding
that raises my anger and I surprise us both
by banging his hood with my fist.
Give me a break. I've fallen off my bike!
I scare myself a little and turn away
get on and ride, the tears flying.
He passes me then pulls over
in his car. My heart begins
to thump fistlike as he gets out
tidy in his blue suit
and I wave him away.
I'm sorry.
I didn't know you'd fallen.
He asks am I okay
and can he take me home.

What he can feel I don't know
but we are twisted
in the metal of ourselves
a true crash pileup —
my tongue and fist,
his scolding and rebuke,
blue suit then shame.
Will we close or open something?
In a sudden speechless covenant
nothing to exchange.

WHO BELONG TO

Be kind to your self, it is only one
and perishable
of many on the planet.
— ALLEN GINSBERG "Who Be Kind To"

And if you died right now
where would they bury
you, among who? Who belong to?
No synagogue or congregation
no brotherhood, sisterhood, no neighbourhood
plot. So who? Who belong to?

I want to say: Air then.
Dissolve me and fling me there.
Or water. Or any old
earth behind my house
to be dug up by the cats
for peeing in.

And that's OK, I guess.
Those sound fine until
I read about a woman
visiting her father's grave,
him among his friends the Workman's Circle,
about the Chinese-Americans burying their own.

How people rush to get membership
in synagogues just before the holidays
or death. We need a place to rest

when the fear comes. Me,
not a member anywhere. Who
belong to?

But wait. I have cards
to all kinds of organizations.
I am a member everywhere. I am
a member of the League of Canadian Poets,
a member of Ontario Health.
I own a MasterCard
and a coffee card and a library card,
and now sitting here at the Second Cup
with my card stamped again, I wonder
what this will get me later
besides a free one?
Maybe there's a green expanse
of land behind head office
where all us members go
or maybe the poets will bury me
or the librarians.

The last synagogue I went to
will send a reminder for services,
and Master Card will claim
I'm still a part of their family.
Their envelopes will arrive together
and with other letters gather, a paper mass,
push up the lid on my mailbox
so that anyone from the street will notice
how they stand, for me,
a congregation.

HIGHLIGHTS OF THE GALLERY COLLECTION: A TOUR

I. Untitled

You stare at the pile, dumb-eyed.
A sculpture. You're supposed to know this.
Your mind scurries under a guard's chair repeating
the word 'chair' for safety. *Chair. Chair.*

Your eye patrols the room, while your body stays hidden,
gathers titles for clues. Every piece here is called "Untitled."
Give up. Walk out, swearing: *The gallery. Taxes. Ottawa and Art.*
My kids could do it. I could do it. Shrug and surrender, hands up.

And on the way to the exit — past trying, past the guard —
notice a thing in the corner, like a tall building,
a column of green shelves, a mausoleum, a ladder
to the stars and look up, where your eye wants to go

lifted to the air, to where there is no answer and no question,
no thought. Never mind what it is, it's what it does
where the eye goes where the breath goes
how the spine moves upward in imitation to the sky.

II. Mark Rothko: Red and Black

Stand in front of it
feeling something, unspeaking it.
Try to find words to put the painting into,
so your brain can hold it. You want
to relieve yourself of the weight of the painting,
the dense squares layering your body
as you stand, thinking — *with words I could cut*
that canvas square of red, release the blood, yes.

But if you let the pain out
you'd lose the painting
because the painting holds the pain.
The painting, in turn, holds you, says,
stand in front of me,
your body knows this red,
feel it, comfort and anguish,
I am speaking.

III. Comments

A man was arrested for throwing up
on paintings. He said it was
his comment on the art, and was acquitted.

Those white cards in the lobby can hold
a few lines of praise or criticism,
an excited drawing, but no vomit.

How else to convey what matters?
This poem will come and go, a feather in a canyon,
a bit of phlegm brought up and washed off.

A government official in another country,
removed for reciting a poem
in public, will stand again for election
at the site of the offending poem.

What remains of the gesture is its offense
or its thrill, and the next layer's reactions: a palimpsest
of messages, invisible inks that bloom and fade,
requiring the black-light of memory to detect
the thin print of our spit and saliva.

DRY SEASON AT THE MONASTERY: AN INVENTORY

There was the path to the cemetery,
all the stones the same. The maze
of trees around the graves, an inner
hedge of pine an outer one of cedar, trimmed
shoulders hugging the path. Me, the single walker.
There were the raspberry rows behind the maze
almost ripe; the wildflowers clinging
to the garden fence, free for the taking.
There was the tenacious hold of their stems.
There was the statue of Mary on a nearby mound,
the words, *Consolatrix Afflictorum*. There was the sage
pulled fresh from the hill, green like a wing.
There were Saskatoon berries, high up and blue.
A little dry. Not a great season, she said
as she filled my hand. There was
the freshly oiled road, slick and stinking.
The dry one we were on.
There was the dust behind the car and
the rocks flying up. There was the cracking
of the rocks against the glass, the dust like smoke.
There was being alone there and waiting.

A WALLPAPER'S LIFE

1.
First, we showered
a soapy spray onto its scored
pages till they sucked the wet
to melt the glue. It softened,
sagged, we peeled it, tore it down.
Sometimes like a skin, sometimes
like a petticoat flipped back:
it hung upon itself. More garment
underneath required still
more water, steam, more effort.
It wanted to stay up
to hold the wall, itself, in place
and seemed to be the solitary break
between the weather and the house:
a membrane, paper thin, barely
shell enough to keep the contents in.

Each time I peeled, I found beneath
new lines of fault, trajectories of blame,
and whatever care I brought was
not enough. Whole chunks of wall
came down. Ancient seeds
of gravel, crushed, spilled out. I tried
to pat it back — it wouldn't stay.

The seam had opened years before
and worsened in the inner weather.
The hot dry furnace air cracked
my lips, each year they bled a little.
The paper curled and cracked
a vertical smile, decrepit grin
widening jack-o-lantern rot: it went open.
It reacted to new glue with repulsion
tearing back a heaving breath.
The natural moves of age and strain
indicted me to take it down.
Take me down, it wheezed.

Nowhere else to go but slip to blindness
not to see the widening smile, to be
so rich to hire someone else to do the mending;
to be so comfortable with my hands that I'd have
faith and some resilience in repair.

"The more you dig, the more appears,"
my neighbour said, and when he saw
my frightened face, added quick,
"It's just a wall."

Why then a cringe with every scrape?
As if the wall in me could not bear
so much exposure, so much
being seen without my paper.

2.

An old man's body
spread with wounds, brown beneath his suit.
Gouged or bruised, I wasn't sure,
could not get near the howling form.
Saw, then, they were invisible
only I could see them, others saw
a pale, a hairy skin, round and soft.
The old man just patted his chest.
But in the sight of want —
boys on the bridge sniffing paper bags,
a ragged poem, a film with outstretched ribs —
he felt the bruises, winced.

Friends with palsied legs
were asked to *hop up* on tables, tried.
Diseases of the eyes would not
stop crying, wore dark glasses.
Plaster casts of brains altered,
held in cases for preservation
to be studied, covered, not so much by
cabinetry, but designations: formal.

I used to photograph
derelict buildings, homes of other countries.
Dublin ruins, or Havana's.
"Beauty in the ravages," I thought,
but not my ravaged house, my human
shame. This imperfection deep enough
is ugly, or what is felt to be,

disgarded, filed,
forgotten, hidden, wished away.

Where some would see a fixable work-in-progress
I, transfixed by sudden uncovered pain,
and without the confidence or want,
whether — how — to cover it again.

Goods and Services

INSPECTIONS

1. Air

No one breathed
a word, but people began
to get sick in distant parts
of the building. One breast
by the photocopier, testes
at the front desk. Limbs and lymphs
were silently being removed
like swift editing jobs.

And the air vent
that rarely sighed —
when the man on a ladder
held his scanner up to its mouth —

                                went completely still.

2. Food

One part of my brain is meat, the other animal:
one part in clear plastic wrap, the other carried
between cars on the shoulders of men.
The cows were lowing down Christie St. like a subway
screech to the slaughterhouse. Radiant smell now gone:
a hole dug for condos. The animal part of my brain
wants to leave a sign for tenants. I remember
Ireland, a pre-Christmas party
and the butcher, red-faced, sat grumbling.
I left, saw in back of his car a curly sheep standing.
In the alley behind the grocery, two deer in a sky-
blue trailer, their knees broken to fit.
I couldn't help covering my face:
their open eyes. Blood from the trachea.
No inspectors is normal in alleys.
What do you expect, the little stores with their
hunters? It's November, the season, and the boy
by the trailer, hiding. *My mother hates this.*
Out front this store has one face, now
there are front and back faces.

My brain goes it alone, tries to be body-less.
One inspects, the other cries like a cow.
My brain goes to a therapist: worries.
She says 'go up to the third floor
a woman does massage there, you have a body.'
Afterward I am filled, illuminated, ample:
my brain and my body in the same house.

Now Christmas, my husband buys a bird,
the head still on, says
'This is what I wanted all my life, to face up
to the truth of what I'm eating. Thank you, bird.'
Its eyes and beak closed, peaceful,
bagged like a body in a crime show freezer,
its long neck bowed.

3. Retirement Homes, Tattoo Parlours

meet in the same phonebook
blue page. What they have in common
is where they fall in the alphabet,
in the dating game of government inspections,
together under the same watchful eye, alcohol swab and glove,
bottled handwash, signs of care.

A number written in a chart has its intentions;
three letters on the sidewalk is an unknown promise;
blue tattoo on a breast for love
or survival, the blue ink
of radiation. The gown, surgery green,
backless. A courtroom drama
of inspectors sniffing instruments,
cheese cubes at the mayor's New Year's Day levée,
the tattoo artist, the lady resident,
the warm scarf at her neck, the skin under it;

the numbered arm, revealed, touched. Wrinkled. Blue.
The body. The belly of the city at the legislature
half its constituents below. Windows facing
south. Swollen ankles of the city, unbalanced, trying.
Skin pierced. The planned,
the chaotic body, infected,
beautiful. The syringe of mistakes
in rainbow colours. The syringe of clear wishes.
The red underside. The solid city pavement
on which homes and parlours rest,
the bright blue hospital shuttle buses, carrying people
like chaperones.

THE CAMERA STAYS

His photographs are structures:
every frame a building
and each with three floors.

Three floors up
three rooms wide:
photograph, a stanza.

And inside each some detail
starts to fail, a necessary trait
threatens to jump.

He says, *I want to see
the human in the stone,
the banisters like teeth.*

He records the facts of walls,
the shame of windows blacked
like three eyes shut. A column cracked

a

        tooth

SIX O'CLOCK NEWS

In the faces of politicians:
the welcome smile.
In their voices:
the coached baritone,
the slowed speech of one
who expects an audience, the deliberate
syllables of *information*.
Prepared looks on their faces
even the women look shaved,
their cheeks barely moving
the windows of their eyes
all clouds.

Their work
demands years of practice,
to keep the unexpected
getting through.

I have seen one labour
under heavy lights
and not crack. His skin stretched
tight with what he's not saying,
what he desires coming through closed lips
coming through.

Most politicians choose
a look and stay
with it.
Some say "Dumb" or "Tough."
To see one genuinely surprised is rare.
Safety: the blank face
that draws us there.

THE OVEN WINDOW

Just to watch something rise,
and be fragrant, to watch the oven window
after the TV images of what fell
and the imagined stench. Vanilla.
Egg yellow. Flour. The white
heads, the grey
with an arm in it. Recipe:
tattooed shoulder, ringed hand. A woman
cries out: Something is missing inside.
The impossibly wrong flux
the blood, a chasm

                                            sky

ground
an opening in her chest she has to jump
as though blood itself has to make a leap,
and she, looking for where to flow now, how,
what to flow into.
I look for the pan to hold
the batter. Grease of life. Oil.
Another ingredient. Salt. Tartaric acid.
Please. Sponge, angel. Something round, ordinary.

WEATHER

A softness
comes through me like a wave
laps across the room to the woman
there, and she feels it,
soothed.

Sometimes a sharp salt breeze
comes up fierce in my chest,
rushes out in a gale. Sometimes I know
where it's heading and sometimes

it has its own intention, upsets
all her castles, clears the beach.
When it meets her own strong wind, the room
lights up in storm and rain falls on the carpet.

On a calm day, there is
so much space the walls fall down

and we can see more.

Sometimes I am fog. Dense and thick.
Can hardly make out the figure
over there in the chair. She is fog too.

At times a bird in the room
with clear eyes, sharp beak. Lights

on the bookshelf, sees the oil slick on the shore,
sees the shiny pebble, picks it up.

Sometimes if I hold that stone steady a long time,
she will take it. Study its colours
blue, no, green. Weather permitting,
they shimmer.

CANADA TRUST

Everyone with a badge on their chest, a name dimly perceived.
An old man with the tag: *war, wound of the heart.*
A boy of eight: *fondled by grandmother, shame.*

A woman's tag, *forgotten.*
She's in line at the bank. The teller's name
pinned above his own counting hands: *ignored.*

They look away,
the way two shoppers meet
at a bulk bin, salty hands

the way a man comes out of a dressing room,
pant cuffs rolled three times, waiting for
approval, and you are passing there

the way a young man tells it all
to a doctor, then sees her in a flirty skirt downtown
and she sees him seeing her

the way two old men sit on opposite porches
not speaking for thirty years, watching each other,
the way they don't speak.

The teller checks her signature under infrared light.
They look down together waiting to exist. The signature
runs between them like a river, like a strand of hair.

AT THE OFFICE

We have them.
Though not necessarily
visible. By the watercooler.

Not like mushrooms, or worms
after rain or crocus heads in spring.
Not the lush or dangerous plant life
of the forest. More like a hum, a whisper.

One has migraine headaches
that wrench her from day; another's
inner ear gets thrown, and nightly
swims him in green vertiginous waves.

There's one whose lungs afford too much material.
Watery and raw each January, she's drowned
by March. One has bled burnt blood
for months.

Another bleeds the bright fresh red of cut,
skin linings no one can see without help.
This one's heart hurts, keeps her up
the feel of fire in her chest.

Each one of us has a part that's weak.
We wake in the morning checking
for pain, cracks in the lining, breaks
in normal and for whatever holds the rest together

and we come to work again.

BLOSSOM

While I'm here I'll do the work.
And what's the Work?
To ease the pain of living.
— ALLEN GINSBERG "Memory Gardens"

Things I've taught:
Words mainly. But also a few hands
to bake bread, print photographs.

I'm no mother.
I want to say to children:
We are left alone a lot.
And there's no telling
where the help will come from.

I aim to work
inside the daily body. The way bewilderment
lives inside one not taught to speak or thank,
the way panic blossoms in one gone blank
who's supposed to know. The way, I hope,
bread somewhere is leavening,
or branches bursting into trees
radiating evidence in the darkest of darkrooms.

SUMMONED

All my life I rehearse
the witness box.
I am the female Mr. K., waiting
for the knock, hell,
I *am* the knock.
Police in the street raise alarms in my chest.

So here's the knock
and I know what it's about. My neighbour
hit two years ago and on that night
I heard a thump and when they came to ask me
what I heard
I said *a thump*, and that was that.

My father'd ask me more —
names and fathers' names, what they did
and where they worked, and what time home —
and when that voracity was slaked
he'd eat his dinner, and I could rest.

Here's my walk-on part, at last.
Here's the summons. Here's the Crown,
long and thin in grey, lipstick black, she looks
a worried bird; and here's the short
defense attorney in flaming robes
and there, up there the judge who smiles
a generous, enormous smile

as though to welcome me into her house and I suppose,
it is her house.

I have to swear to tell the truth.
Choice of Bible, old or new, or personal assertion.
Personal, to mean that I could guarantee the truth
and not a book. Not an outside god, no other
mother, father, just this *Yes*.

The defense begins. She asks my profession,
where I live and what I heard. I answer short
and when she wants more detail,
give what I can and to the rest
say, *I don't know*. She keeps asking
what I did the day before and where was I,
and sitting here two years
later, all I say is, *I don't know*.

It rises like a chorus in me, like a chant
goes on and on, the solid song
of *I don't know*,
a blazing, spectral truth,
baptismal inner dance
which in this moment has to be,
and is, enough.
Inside this house,
the public lung,
all our defences rest.

NEIGHBOURHOOD

I.
The sun colouring into garden lamps, ice cream in a bowl,
Grand Marnier. Slow June night.
Behind my neighbours' fence, we talk and drink.
Noise on the street and others outside come close.

I am here. Begin. Gather a neighbourhood
call it *mine*. Begin: beget or be gotten.
Flies around garbage gather; a mosaic of broken plates
each a piece of wall.

Memories walk through one another like nights.
Through me. I'm gathering nouns
where we overlap, where I recede and return.
The subjectivity of it.

Of the grocery store, someone says,
such a dirty floor. Bottleflies inside the fridge,
the store is open whenever you need a coke.
And upstairs: Vito's house.

My neighbour talks of taking over this corner store,
he makes a grand café on the balcony, tables with tea lights
in summer. But that's where Vito lives and no one's
moving or dying yet, and I salute you, Vito.

Vito and his wife survey their lot.
Flowers from his plastic pots lavish

the balcony rail. Purple and red. Reds drape
his yard. Tomato plants.

One son lives at home, sick maybe. Things erupt.
Sometimes police outside
don't seem to know what to do
and drive away.

Vito walks the sidewalk on a poor hip,
pear body careful. Stretches over his
homemade fence to prune a fig.
'So-so,' his answer to all questions.

His wife waves and smiles.
I've never heard her speak.
Peering through the slats in my blind, I catch the eye
of Vito's wife, peering through hers.

II.
On the street something is happening.
Our car's been smashed three times.
Thunderbird set on fire, 4 AM flames from a window
a woman hiding. *She knew the guy.*

A boyfriend in the alley and a father
with a blue company shirt who says
hello to me with a kissy face.
One morning rice in the street

piles of it, not from throwing,
but like a bag punctured or

a salt truck leaking rice.
Another day something like blood

spattered down Christie, hoping it's paint,
what if it ends at my door? The dogs
sniff and howl on the thin side
of the wall

want to go out. The tight-jeaned woman up
and down stairs, taxi waiting every night
at 10, radio on again at 4. Who is
the man doing laundry in mirrored glasses?

Or the boy moving toward home
in a medicated shuffle?
Who is the woman with the narrow face,
body of a stick I see with her daughter?

The corner store sends its garbage
with the wind; casts
its scrap in the yards, absorbed by
gardens. Torn lottery tickets,

chip bags and coffee cups,
flecks of styrofoam like imported snow.
We bend to pick it up. Bend and chat.
Avoid or link eyes. Come together in clumps:

III.
on Sunday mornings Korean families
jostle for parking, their voices from the nearby church
come at my window, high and firm and beautiful.
Gone again by noon to restaurants on Bloor St.

'This is happy Lord day.' Others come
to Moises where they can get goat but not eggplant because
'*Only a few Italians buy it*' and this is a Portugese store.
While I go in for broccoli, I'm not who they have in mind.

People fall together in groups and I not akin
to any — not Chinese, Korean, Portugese —
but to some partially dissolved contingent. Jewish.
Or Jewish-ish. Like an emulsion: dispersed or distinct

buoyant, blended or suspended.
One lone yarmulke bobs down the street and I'm surprised.
Hear him talk Yiddish to his three-year-old daughter.
Recognize it like a prayer, understand not a word.

Fall together in groups
then apart into selves.
Who am I as I head to Kin's? As I hunger
for the shiny red chicken balls?

IV.
In the backyard something is mingling. The visiting
black cat with velvet collar sits on my cushioned lawnchair
waiting for her closeup, then pisses behind the lettuce.
Reggae drifts.

Neighbours on one side build fences for their dog,
on the other, grow lupins
and fish in ponds. The tenor is practising scales again,
and the kids wail, *shut the fuck up.*

Everything my parents fought to keep out
is getting in. So that sitting
in my backyard on a tar-scented night
these sounds come uncorralled, make a mess.

Speed mocks the sign of the turtle who models a slow
a quiet neighbourhood.
Verbal scrawl like chalk on a wall,
the muscle cars screeching their names.

V.
Friday night at Blockbusters then Loblaws:
the annoying people behind me at the video store
are the same ones behind me at the grocery.
'Don't call me stupid,' she says to her son,

'and don't call yourself stupid either. That's stupid.'
Loving it, hating it and kin to it. Loblaws.
The great flattener, cultural hog
snorting up everything in its path.

Shelves of Thai green curry and Kosher Fajita sauce.
You can stand in the aisles forever.
Go there to get out of winter or the unbreathable
summer, go there instead of a movie 'cause it's free.

No one will ask questions.
The young Chinese man in line has a cart piled high
with 2 litre bottles of coke. A five-itemed woman
groans then smiles: 'he's got his own store.'

How the community eats itself.
Still, he talks to no one and no one
asks why he wants that much of anything.
Loving it because no one cares.

Safe. Can't make a mistake: a man
at the Harbord Bakery asks proudly for a *challah*
pronounced like cheese. I take a shoe to a dressmaker.
'But it's canvas,' I plead. They laugh, wave me off.

In Loblaws each country's got its own shelf,
and whoever shops here knows
the rules. The workers wear beige and behave.
Same coke as outside but outside no manager.

Outside in Nick's shoe repair, three old men with soft faces sit
while I wait for Nick who says 'Yes, a patch. From the inside.'
Another old man in the back. Like a leather-smelling coffee bar,
a hangout for old Italian men Wednesday 10 AM.

Outside Nick decides what to wear, when to close.
Everyone plays by different rules.
Ones with cockroaches or cigarette ash dropping
onto the meat, children on laps while owners press the cash.

It's cars on fire and windshields busted
the neighbour out in the street like a shot
sweeping up broken glass. It's the hood ornament breathing down
from the Jaguar dealership one block north.

It's women in skin-licking pants
serving cappuccino to their boyfriends.
It's the rattle of the train from the tracks behind Dupont,
the punch in the chest of a car woofer in summer

and the Portugese sports announcer
racing the ball, reaching to trail his one long vowel
and you know what he's saying even if you don't. He goes
'o o o o o o o o o o o o o o o o o o o o o o o o o o o o o o o o o'

the long line of his voice like a baseball or horse
in the distance of another yard, one yard after another, one
clothesline after another, colours, whites, rags and clothes
that don't resemble clothes, socks like tubes

and shirts like flags, inarticulate shapes, flap
continuing from one yard to the next entangled
in grapevines, onto balconies and branches
bright day noise fading to a close, to night

to the sound of the Christie bus sighing
to a stop because this is a quiet neighbourhood,
that's what the sign says.
                              And I want it, all

even the underfoot rice, fling of paint
and blood or not the blood but even what I hate
I love. The woman next door who'll take me to court.
The patriarch, Vito, vanishing to the suburbs.

All of it gathering in me, the accumulated slugs and embraces
of one cross-hatched set of roads.
That day Christie Street was resurfaced, peeled back
and everyone walked in the underworld.

Big yellow dinosaur diggers and no one drove.
Everyone stepping down
into the street that was suddenly lower and wider
as though we could walk out farther and deeper on our own.

Original Christie recalled like a tide so far out
it was nowhere and everyone careful on the unrolled earth
waiting for Christie to be replaced but also glad for:
corduroy? corn rows? gravel? land?

Each with our different word, a venn diagram of overlapping
eyes. And we walked in the road as at a carnival,
those dinosaurs like rides, waiting and still,
the favour of walking with unknown neighbours

the possibility that we were free of danger
and the freedom of being with complete strangers,
complete, standing like me in the understreet,
loopy, recalibrated, altered world.

ASYLUM

                    She says, "I stopped
going to therapy to buy an antique sideboard,
and three of my lesbian friends have gone straight."

                    We are on our way
to a play, a version of a version of a version
of *Faust*, a version of a version of Gertrude Stein.

                    Strolling through
the grounds of Queen Street Mental Health,
we come upon a wall two hundred years old.

                    She says,
"I am so fluid it scares me." Stands on the path between
the roamers inside, and the wall, sturdy, partial, unreliable.

WORK

How does it happen?
A person gives 43 years to a place.
43 years. To a job.
It happens
one coffee at a time, one bagel
toasted. One pen at a time, one typewriter
then one computer. It happens one
mimeographed sheet of paper at a time
and one paper shredded. One
never-quite-up-to-par-actually-pretty-lousy
photocopier at a time. It happens one
more coffee at a time and one more
face at the desk. One story at a time,
one tear, many. One rage
at a time, one thank you. Somebody
else's arrival and somebody else's
retirement. Somebody's baby, somebody's
death. It happens and then
one more coffee, one more 2 o'clock
in the afternoon. One more lunch
eaten at the busy desk. One more year
of winter walks to work, one more
year of raw throats. One more meeting, yet
another meeting. It happens. Somehow.
A person spends 43 years of a life.
She gives and spends. Makes a life.
43 years. One at a time.

Then how do we say goodbye?
One meeting at a time,
counting down to the last.
The last lunch. The last time I say:
see you in the morning.
We count. Driving ourselves, each other
crazy with goodbyes, last times.
The minutes fill up with goodbyes.
We say goodbye with everything.
One story at a time. One tear at a time.
One at a time. One of us
at a time.

Skin and Bones

NICE POEMS

I want to write nice poems,
poems in which no one dies
no bodies are turned inside out
for observation, no
stories spilled like guts
after salmonella
or kept fastidiously in.

I want to write poems
in which the helplessness
of all the nurses, doctors,
social workers, school teachers, custodians,
parents and children, does not feature.
Where every person wanting a sling,
a pill, a letter, a word, advice, a remedy,
a salve, an ear, a transplant —
physical or emotional —
a chair to sit on, a table to bleed on,
a bed to lie on when none are
available, or if available,
no one with any energy left to dispense them,
doesn't feature.

I want to write a poem where
none of this exists.
But this isn't it.

OLD MONK, TEENAGE GIRL

I don't want struggle but struggle is in me.
It says: 'I am the struggle. *Listen.*'

And because I close my eyes, inventing peace,
it struggles more: squeezes out at the edges
the skin around bra straps, squeezes
around the edge of sleep inside my eyelids
before they open. Calmed by the obstacle
of making dinner, it reveals itself in the dishes.

Cranky and cheeky: the old monk yelling,
I am hungry, in the church. Just wants food.
The girl in the tight top and shortest
skirt. No warning will defy her, her body
yelling, *hey baby, look at this.*

I am the struggle, let me out. I am the struggle
fast and furious. I am the god-hunger and the lust,
the howl beneath the articulate phrase,
the scream that closes the book, the hollow
wordless mouth just behind the one
with answers. I am the serrated edge
of contact, rocking into each
the unpeaceful, the purr's opposite,

groaned like death across the desert or like birth
haveme haveme haveme. Yours to pound

into the drum of days, into the quick white night.
I am the monk in your throat scream in the church
and his admonishing maid. I am the strap
around the back of the bra and the skin that refuses.
I am the girl in the skirt, wiggling before the audience
of boys and her mother's voice. I am that voice of panic
dropping out of the phone into the empty booth;
the monk forgotten, the girl on the run and this time,
the one that hears them.

SKIN AND BONES: THE MEN

The Gown

After the procedure
he stood beside the hospital bed
and dropped his gown. Whatever
that the curtain was open and he was naked.
His body was absent-minded, suddenly
his heart unleashed and went home.
Thank you, nurses.

He dispatched countless telephone calls
filaments of love,
apologies and declarations,
closed his eyes and dreamed himself
a highway, with exits, tributaries —
how, like a dog shivering in sleep,
all his limbs trembled.

The Son

Today you're an old man.
Clean shaven.
Not the leathered cheeks
of the man carrying cabbages
across the street. Not the prickly
husk on the face of his son, carrying
apples. Yours is a smooth face.

When you shaved the beard years ago
I was shocked to see: your mother's chin.
The flaps of your cheeks suddenly soft.
As though this chin might bring a new man,
gentler. But the razor showed how
little exposure your skin had ever known,
how like a baby under it all.

Mad

"Get over your jealousy, Mother,"
the boy shouts after asking
if she'd seen Jesus. Because she hadn't.

"Get over your jealousy that I can
refuse weddings and funerals, that I
see God, in daylight.

I wear the word 'Saviour'
on my jacket. Spray it
on the wall by my car.

The anger in your face,
I know what it is. You wish for this freedom.
Get over your jealousy." The boy walks away.

The anger in her face is a red knot
of skin, sirens on police cars
a tiny moon of blood in the white of her eye.

In her ears
the only speech is this
one-eyed rant.

Her breath wears a chronic necklace
of sorrow, the sound of his shuffle.
The ping ponging of her own

heart like a nut inside its shell
ready to open,
ready to crack.

The boy grows large, takes over the street.
His mother moves out, leaves
food in the freezer.

The Soldier

I went to them. I took the plane, reported
to the customs agents, "visiting the museum
of the medical." My urge to see the humans tucked
and sewn, the eyes of wax, the colons grown
to forty feet and their accomodating bellies,
anencepholated skulls and those who never separated
from their brothers. I went and saw
the mostly men, though first recorded electroshock
a woman and deemed successful,
a wall of skulls collected, priced by crime.
And walking through the catalogue of bodies
felt no heart but then a note: the doctor
delivered newborn with a scissors;
the skull of a soldier who died of suicide by gunshot
because of weariness of life; that face
of the man with the swollen colon, shrivelled, waiting
for a cure. Walking back to my hotel
all I could do was cry and wonder why I came
to this Victorian horror show for scholars
and for mockers and felt at home.
Paid money, flew to another city, country,
like a person seeking roots, my genealogy
though unrelated. A wall of skulls.
A display of pain I lay no special claim to
except when I have been that freak and wished
someone would visit me and let their eyes get hot
and wet and melt like wax.

The Suit (1)

Fat but extremely clean
well manicured thumb,
the whole hand. Entire
surface of beard
trimmed like a lawn.
No to scraggle on cheeks.
Hair, likewise, kempt.
Shirt around barrel
chest, white.
Not too thin to reveal
old man nipples. 100%
cotton. Pressed by drycleaner,
folded, cardboard. Suit of fine
wool. Pinstripe elegant
grey on grey, fine pink threading.
No gangster stripes. The up
stripes must meet the down.
Those stripes on other suits who
miss each other, fire off
into unmatched lines,
like the criss-cross of badly sewn scars,
draw attention to themselves.
The possibility of shame.
On each jacket sleeve,
a legitimate button hole
opens. A moment of forgiveness.
War, even when it dithers, is reliable, poised.
Cuffs of shirt emerge, shrugged
and showing gold links. Manicured nails
round, pink.

Eugene

Uses ingredients like language.
No word is too expensive.

Six bottles of red wine
reduced to its essence.

The bath-size bowl of salad greens
each leaf cleaned, dressed.

The Gown

He stood beside the hospital bed
and dropped his gown. Whatever that
the curtain was open, and he was naked.

The Names of Chocolates

He kept in his wallet a list
of chocolates his wife adored

Laura Secord Preferences:
Gloria
Laurette

then a note to remind him:
Half the purchase in French Crisp

close to his body,
beside a photograph
the blond boy of four
the daughter's son, he called *Sunshine*

★

who found
this wallet among their things
the picture of his cloudless self

and his name, returning to his tongue
like a gift of chocolate, sweet in the cheek
of his mouth.

SKIN AND BONES: THE WOMEN

Beautiful People with Hemorrhoids

People in dresses and jewels
line up on the red carpet.
Their arms do not swing.
Their bodies are a sign of wealth.

They wear collarbones
as protection,
higher than reproach.

To say,
*Doesn't everyone need
someone to feel better than?*

To scan for frailty —
to defeat, to protect.

Under their gowns
they are bleeding.

Vigilantly sheathed
spasms of life. Tender
and inflamed.

Anonymous

The ice that sealed the compartment is pried off
in one satisfying door-shaped chunk. Once inside,
a frozen liver is prodded bloodless, two
forgotten kidneys, thawed and smelled.
And in the night the motor, like a heart,
keeps rattling.

In the morning, clean and silent
only white walls. The old refrigerator is left outside,
its door removed to protect children.

Shivering past, a woman pulls her coat
around her, like a curtain in a hospital
no one can enter.

Highlights of the Gallery Collection: A Tour

IV. *The Big-Breasted Tour Guide & The Disappearance*
    of the Big-Breasted Tour Guide

'Breasts.' That's what you're thinking.
You're not thinking, *Adoration*
of the Shepherds. You're thinking, 'Breasts.'
It doesn't matter that this tour is "Highlights
of the European Collection." We're talking
big names here: Rembrandt, Rubens. *Elevation*
of the Cross on Good Friday and you're thinking, 'breasts.'

The tour guide does not say, "Do they look like mine?"
She's not really there, just a filter: gives you
permission to look, look at everything, see everything
as long as it stays in the frame. Not her.
Whatever you do, don't look at her.
She is a guide: the breasts are on the wall.

Jane

A person gives 43 years to a place
of work. To a job. 43 years.
One coffee at a time (cream),
one bagel (jam). One pen at a time (it leaked),
one typewriter, then one computer. One
mimeographed sheet of paper
and one paper shredded.
One story at a time (her brother dies),
one tear, many. One rage (grasping),
one thanks (a card with sun).
Arrival and retirement.
Baby (premature),
death. It happens
and then
one more coffee, one more 2 o'clock
in the afternoon. One more lunch
at the busy desk. One more year
of winter walks to work, one more
year of raw throats. One more meeting,
yet another (who will keep
the minutes now). It happens.
A person spends 43 years of a life.
She gives and spends. Takes
down the photographs of wildness,
the Ontario lakes where, lunchtimes,
she swam up, takes a life
off the walls and leaves
an office, a central reservoir
a pool of Jane
to remain behind her.

The Suit (2)

"Before she died she bought a blue suit at Holt Renfrew.
She knocked on my door wearing the suit
with a wide brimmed hat.
She said, *I just wanted you to see me in this suit.*
The next time you see me looking this good, I'll be laid out.

Loud and vain. Her mouth always open
and that great horizon of teeth
now a bruised yellow,
illness and too much tea.
Bald under that hat.

In childhood's truth her white hair
puffs up like stiff, whipped mashed potatoes.
With a décolleté and large gold things
hanging in between. She was so short
she was all breasts, huge spreading lips
a laugh like a jab. Wild aunt near my school,
an unparent, phantasm alone. The door left ajar
in her bathroom so she could make comments and watch TV.

I worked one summer in her tyrannical
Crescent St. boutique. Pattern of snake sashayed
around my neck. Tongue flick of life. It was possible.
She scared me with her shamelessness, like a guide.
I never thanked her. I knew of no one
she loved privately. She slept
in rumours.

The next time I saw her, she was laid out
head back, eyes closed like she'd swallowed the sun,
and she was wearing that blue suit."

Goodbye To All The Rooms

She thanked the shower for its heat in winter,
its ferocious strength. Told her bedroom
she would miss it: first place she created,
indeterminate colour between peach
and pink. Burnt a picture of her old dead self
in the kitchen sink. Tore up all the rules and threw
some Tibetan dust off the balcony, thinking:
Where is home now that this isn't?
Whose arms?
Which pocket holds the fear?
I've been a person in a whole body
who lives only in the skin.
Before you can leave a place
you must say goodbye to all the rooms.
You must say hello to them.
I'm ready now.
This body with its curves. This mind
with its angles. These greedy arms.

A Parade of Gowns

I was sitting in the waiting room
Lakeshore Boulevard, in the silence of a Sunday.
The only sound: air pushed through vents,
pumped, repumped.

My friend's mother had had a heart attack;
half her heart was dead
though she was still alive.
Such a small heart left.

Another I knew went
for surgery Tuesday. General
anaesthetic. Woke up shaven,
in the care of her partner. These are stories.

A parade of women carried pillows
through the hospital.
Went home without
their breasts.

On the surface things look fine,
new breasts are offered.
A buried instrument rusts out.
An organ fills.

The instrument is detected
and dug up like a time capsule.
People run away from each other
in shock. Don't tell your stories, they yell.

The effects are studied and displayed
in a great art exhibition
of our mistakes, lonelinesses
and the staff are thanked, at least that.

People have to keep working here
walking the halls
and no one knows how to talk about it.
But the volunteers.

They our elders tend to ramble, they
are free, safe from suit, they know
they are the keepers of the stories
deposited in passing. When we tell them.

Everybody's Birds

I am sitting with my sister
in the small orthodox synagogue
the women's section, behind
the men, her husband. A year today
their daughter buried.

Enter the substantial scroll wrapped
in a fine wine velvet mantle
on which their daughter's name is sewn in gold.
Her date of birth and five years later, death.

And at the front, the husband's
called to make the prayer
that brings the Torah home. Invited
to stand and hold the rounded book.

In his arms
the girl, his daughter, wrapped and sacred
cradled. He holds her there beside the ark.
The velvet coat against his cheek.

He is being held there too, upheld
by men in shawls, swaying in all directions.
Just as my sister, among the watching
women, sits alone.

★

Nothing in her lap but hands
and only hers. She sits and
nothing tells her what to do.
The public work of grief is done;

the grief itself, unheld,
uncovenanted, alone.

*

One year later: the paper-weighted belly.
Another breath inside her breath
pulls down, swelling
the gravity of so much risk.
And he comes out alive.
Grows up to be the one wild one,
grows up to be six
and chasing birds on the beach
till the lonely sand man bellows back
stop chasing away my birds
and the boy, in protest, yells
they're not your birds, they're everybody's birds.

And she, his frightened mother, turns back astounded
as though he'd yelled into the face of the stranger
into the empty ark, the ocean, into her face
it's not your grief, it's everybody's grief
and felt something lift, delirious, dispersing
back among the congregants, circulating,
carried
like the birds, everybody's birds.

Public Works

PUBLIC WORKS

Out of an ancient confusion, comes a strategy:
look up Public Works.
Want to know what's mine, what is a work?
Make a list.

I use roads, don't I? Put out garbage.
Parking tickets like cryptic letters
are left on my windshield.
And once the hydro man waved to me
from his box in the air.
A string of lights across the country.

*

Make a list.
Libraries, of course, indoor pools where I inhale water,
the heritage building where I married, kissed.
Its living gas lights, sweeping drapes, buildings
where officers send envelopes through chutes
to bodies that deliver them,
public servants at the door address me
by name or genera or occupant,
send me to the school to cast my ballot
in cardboard privacy
or summon me to witness
what I've witnessed,
make public a thump through shared walls,
broadcast truth for the sake of possible bedroom peace

(did anyone get a map
that depicts the trajectory of a summons
before and after it reaches you?).
These constellations that claim me suddenly
like a pothole, a diagnosis sent in the mail.

*

How did I miss this?
Afraid to see the bloated growth, offices
polished then demolished, ignored the bars on Danforth
with the patrons' punched eyes, barren gas stations,
their underground pipes requiring
too much attention to be attended to. Tax forms, bills,
councillors' and ministers' happy pamphlets in the mail,
phonebooks, pleas to donate accumulate
as though I have to greet them all, take in the works,

the electric grid running wired through my veins, sewage
pipes muscling down with their shit, transit working
its worm in a map of arteries, and the phone lines
with their recycling demands,
tiny red lights beaming off my pupils
(the inspector says, *this outlet is not grounded,*
the ceiling here is held together by paint,
if a man like me were upstairs I'd come through),
registering the system and blowing my fuses.

The way a child cannot say no:
no more food, no more talking

for just this minute and becomes too full,
just this breath of air where one muscle,
heart or knot of brain can
make its own connection, rhythm;
not be rammed with shot
and shut down.

*

The mailman stares into the mouth of his bag, annoyed,
says, *I'd like to know who sorted this mail.*
I did, he grins. I am quiet.
A self-contained universe,
each of us, door-to-door.
We don't know what we do.

*

Call me one thousand times, the inspector says
and I want to, want to ask how, of the world,
and don't.

*

Each month a new group of men in high-visibility vests
gather in the middle of the road
stare up at the wires (*high voltage*)
or fish down into the sewer with a polaroid.
And when I ask, muster it to ask, they all go dumb
(*the concrete pole is splitting*)

as though I've broken intimacy
will tell their secrets and I apologize
but I just want to know
(*they will plant a cedar pole, wood is good,*
absorbs vibrations) as though no civilian or woman
has ever before asked what they are doing.
Cleaning, one said.
Is something blocked?
Like washing your face, you do it,
don't you, even when nothing's wrong?
How the annoyed response invites my silence.
To want an answer, to brave the look
a question gets:
to keep standing
undoes everything I thought
about safety.

     *

When did I train
myself toward words or things I could ingest?
Ice cream cones. Loneliness. The small fact
of the mailbox on the corner. The single
mailbox with its letters
but not its letterbomb.
I was privileged to be dumb.
Or like some bombed out shelter,
I was empty.
Did not have to know,
could wonder through, concubine

or princess smiling colonized or scared,
deferring to some greater order
I would not understand and did not try.
If evil is a willful coma, it was close,

a quintessential femme fatale and fatal,
who makes a choice not to know because
to know would mean to fight
the ones who feed you.
So just go blank go blank
till all the voices blend like one
and no distinction, till all the buildings
blur or fade to shapes of pretty light and shadow
likewise parliament become a nothing.

*

How long does a person have to be dead
and how long trusting? Handing a self
over, saying *Here hold this*.
How long till I got tired
of my life on the bench, and all the people
going by, clouds. How long to feel real?
What is work?

In the real world
they say, meaning, *mine*.
In the real world there is just the one way,
else all is chaos and loss, rage, abandon.
In the real world meaning this particular textbook.

What a small corner I backed into saying no
silently blanking blinking no, disappearing (no)
only in the small galleries climbing
ladders of yes, paintings and sculptures of unacknowledged
yes and then books of yes, holding them
like talismans, guides in the dark, backing out of the real world
backing into the world, real.

*

A possible trust: if you know you exist
you don't have to hang on to it. You're just there
lightly in among the electricity and wiring and recycling,
neighbours with their lawns maintained
and yours patchy, in among the delivered newspapers
and the ones undelivered raised to faces on subways.
You don't recognize words but there's the same photograph
of the missing girl.
You are there among the dollar stores changing hands
faster than dollars, and they exist too,
short dollar-store lives, imagined fortunes mourned.
There too among the seen women with swollen lips, eyes sunk
at patio tables along the east Danforth which you never saw
before. (Do they see you? Can they?) What gets noticed
now that you exist too is only everything.
Before, the subcontracted sections of the world
were your provenance, you thought,
as though doled out in crumbs
by someone you couldn't see or could only see
like an emperor's photograph on a high wall.
Giving you to eat, birdlike:

be grateful but not responsible. Not charged but charged.
How the eye goes blank as the mind says 'not this not this.'
Saying 'if I see, then what?'

That fear: to hold the small crumbs of grief
and not look up.
At least I have this, the voice says.

That fear: to look up and be confused,
a small fizz in the head,
and be seen to be confused. And a madness,
a flood of answers comes suddenly, an avalanche
like snow. So now there is that small fizz
beneath a mountain and not one breath
for the confusion, gift itself, to fizzle.

That fear of revealing a mess.

Holding on to the tiny crumbs of poetry, private
conversations, sweet food, sadness:
these cannot be answered and taken away.

The loss of everything else

that corner so small you back into, that refusal:
where you live

that fear of the threshold

that fear of being cancelled.

*

That bicycle ride into the city only for ice cream,
to enjoy the small crumb, sweet drop and then
the flash, almost pornographic: the Legislative Buildings
are nearby around the circle and you've
never seen them, never noticed, never
really looked. Get on your bike
and round it round the crescent called
Queen's Park you've heard forever like two syllables
now full of building and steps and tourists.
You stand behind not understanding
their language, being with them,
confused as they are, existing.

*

I stand in front of the Parliament Buildings one day in May
trying to remember a thing
that will connect me to its crushing structure
before I begin to go down under
pull myself from the brink
saying 'not this time.' Read
in the blessed *Self-Guided Tour*
"308 members sit in the house" and imagine one

from another province, a town out west,
the prairies or the rockies, with a liquor store
and a real estate window. Picture some man
or woman (wins!) gets elected and walks
the corridor, breathes "Can't believe I'm here."
Shoes touch the shiny floor. Member
of Parliament. Voice in the House.

And feeling like a boy, awed but not excluded,
find a face to take me in, a human partner
in my mind to walk through halls to where
there is a desk
a pen a telephone a line — to begin —
find, for one young minute,
that naiveté that I missed —
when I went straight into dismay.

*

You can't reject what was never offered —
as though the world belonged to someone else.
But isn't everyone entitled to a guide in the universe?

*

Holding my paper tour, an introduction,
I find another story, one toe in, look up.
The tower, 1915: how the bell rang
while the Parliament Buildings burned
through three hours' fire it rang,
then at its last midnight stroke, crashed.

You can feel that, can't you,
that plunging bell of flame?
Where everything stopped
had to start again?

*

We bought a house. Beneath it, thunder.
Our neighbour says, *take a bath*,
put your head under the water and the train
is in there with you. In the tub, water
belongs to us, warm, fourteen feet
to the street. Moves in the pipes. Belonging
or not belonging, the new house works,
fitted into the city's plug.
Sewage treatment down hill,
Greenwood station at the top. Snakes
of voltage curl a pole at the back choked
with vines, sympathetic system
of will and pulse. Message. If you think
what it takes to walk or breathe
you'd be paralyzed with astonishment.
The subway, once a place to go, to go
somewhere. Now its constant
animal in my bed rides me
to sleep, wakes me live with the rails.
The brilliant and accomodating body.
Everything gets familiar
until it stops.

         ★

Is he breathing normally?
I don't know. Cut
onions on the chopping board, his finger.
Is the tip gone? Nail gone?
His face gone grey and him falling

all six feet to my height lower
to the wall, rattling the hutch filled with
clean glasses, rattling us to the ground
like some forlorn wrestlers, I am
under him, his head
against the wine rack wire. I lay it down
on the hard tile, his eyes open
but him not there. White eyes.
Calling his name and the receiver
doesn't work, speaker phone 911.
He wakes up sudden, scared,
as though dreaming, falls back down,
head too heavy, she asks if he's breathing,
she's sent the ambulance. But in the
moment between blood and falling we are alone
in this new house
with no walls but a flimsy sky flapping
and the usual human buffers, dissolved.
There are two here and I am the only one awake,
not knowing what peril is and if we're in it.
The ambulance men are red-faced, masked and older,
Scottish accent. *Is he healthy? Awake?*
Blood pressure and saline bag, clean
the wound. It looks small afterward,
only a finger but we needed it,
and in the sun of that blown-open house
those men, Ken and Pete.
One said he liked the furniture, turned round to look
at the room. The other couldn't find his glasses.
Thank you, I said. They helped him to the couch.

Don't leave, I thought, you are now part of my life,
first crisis in the new house. Mazel Tov.
We smashed no glass. I am holding
his hand, the wounded one on the couch.
Alone again our new block stretches further, east to Woodbine
where their station is. Pete and Ken.
Compass point. Plant a flag. Wave. *You're between two*
stations, Ken said. Between. Two stations. Paramedic poles
like tent pegs banged in. We lean carefully.
The subway goes through us but we don't notice.

*

I had a dream that Emily Carr sat in front of our house
painting the hydro pole,
her great knees open and leaning toward the cedar
as though it were still a tree.
All the poles totemic.
Air was colour.
Land was not a verb.
And the sun got up loud as a bell.
The dream, like a work of art,
a realm of power, was private.

In the morning, in the small bedroom window —
while my husband and I fell into the slipstream of our marriage —
I saw a bird on top of that pole. Black.
A raven or a crow?
He saw it too but neither of us said anything
until the next day when we were safely on solid ground, no,
not solid, common; and in the common wonder
could risk seeing what we saw, and ask for a name.

NOTES

"Untitled" is in response to the sculpture of the same name by Donald Judd, at the Art Gallery of Ontario.

The idea, in "Comment," of a poem being a feather in a canyon, came from Eddy Yanofsky, with appreciation.

The sense of trees hugging the path in "Dry Season at the Monastery" was observed by Sandra Campbell and borrowed with thanks.

"The Camera Stays" is after an exhibition of Volker Seding's photographs at the Stephen Bulger Gallery, Toronto, 2001.

"Neighbourhood" is for Rob Norquay and David Townsend.

"Work" is for Jane Phillips.

The museum of the medical, in "The Soldier," is the Mütter Museum, Philadelphia.

"The Names of Chocolates" is from John Edward Armand and for Chris Garbutt.

"The Suit (2)" is dedicated to Lillian Bald.

ACKNOWLEDGEMENTS

I would like to thank the editors of the following journals
and book in which some of these poems appeared: *Ars
Poetica*, *Our Times Magazine*, *Listening with the Ear of the
Heart*.

My thanks to my editor, Beth Follett, who listened for what
I couldn't yet hear, and directed me there.

I am extremely grateful to the Toronto Arts Council, the
Ontario Arts Council and the Canada Council for the Arts
for their support.

This book is for Chris Garbutt.

BETH FOLLETT

RONNA BLOOM has two previously published books of poetry, *Fear of the Ride* (Carleton University Press, 1996, shortlisted for the Gerald Lampert Award for best first book of poetry), and *Personal Effects* (Pedlar Press, 2000). *Personal Effects* has been acquired and translated by the Canadian National Institute for the Blind. Ronna Bloom works as a poetry teacher and psychotherapist. Her poems have been used in anthologies and textbooks and broadcast on CBC Radio. She lives in Toronto.